ICELAND TR. GUIDE 2023

"Unveiling the Charms of Iceland: Your comprehensive Travel Guide 2023 to Hidden Gems, Essential Tips, and Off the Beaten Path Adventures for First-Time Visitors in Iceland"

Thomas J. Webb

All rights reserved. No part of this publication may be reproduced, distributed, or transmitted in any form or by any means, including photocopying, recording, or other electronic or mechanical methods, without the prior written permission of the publisher, except in the case of brief quotations embodied in critical reviews and certain other noncommercial uses permitted by copyright law. While every effort has been made to ensure the accuracy of the information contained in this book, the author and publisher assume no responsibility for errors or omissions, or for damages resulting from the use of the information contained herein.
Thank you for respecting the hard work of the author and publisher. Enjoy your reading experience!

Copyright © Thomas J. Webb, 2023.

Table of Content

INTRODUCTION
- WELCOME TO ICELAND: AN OVERVIEW OF YOUR ADVENTURE
- WHY ICELAND IS THE PERFECT DESTINATION FOR FIRST-TIMERS

CHAPTER 1: PREPARING FOR YOUR TRIP
- PLANNING YOUR ICELAND VACATION: A STEP-BY-STEP GUIDE
- ESSENTIAL ITEMS TO PACK FOR YOUR ICELAND ADVENTURE

CHAPTER 2: EXPLORING REYKJAVIK
- REYKJAVIK: A CITY OF CONTRASTS AND CULTURE

- THE TOP THINGS TO SEE AND DO IN REYKJAVIK

CHAPTER 3: NATURAL WONDERS OF ICELAND
- THE GOLDEN CIRCLE: A ROAD TRIP THROUGH ICELAND'S NATURAL BEAUTY
- EXPLORING ICELAND'S GLACIERS: AN ADVENTURE OF A LIFETIME
- THE NORTHERN LIGHTS: CHASING AURORA BOREALIS IN ICELAND
- RELAXING IN ICELAND'S HOT SPRINGS AND SPAS

CHAPTER 4: BEYOND REYKJAVIK: EXPLORING ICELAND'S REGIONS
- THE WESTFJORDS: ICELAND'S HIDDEN GEM

- THE SOUTH COAST: WATERFALLS, BLACK SAND BEACHES, AND MORE
- THE EASTFJORDS: REMOTE BEAUTY AND SERENITY
- THE NORTH: A LAND OF CONTRASTS AND CULTURE

CHAPTER 5: PRACTICAL INFORMATION FOR YOUR ICELAND VACATION
- GETTING AROUND ICELAND: TRANSPORTATION OPTIONS
- WHERE TO STAY IN ICELAND: A GUIDE TO ACCOMMODATION
- TIPS FOR SAFE AND RESPONSIBLE TRAVEL IN ICELAND

CONCLUSION

- WRAPPING UP YOUR ICELAND VACATION: MEMORIES TO LAST A LIFETIME

INTRODUCTION

Welcome to the ultimate Iceland vacation guide for 2023 - the perfect resource for first-timers looking to explore the stunning landscapes, unique culture, and thrilling adventures that this extraordinary country has to offer. Iceland is a place that truly has it all: from glittering glaciers and cascading waterfalls to volcanic hot springs and the dazzling Northern Lights, this small Nordic island is a true wonder of nature.

If you're planning a trip to Iceland in 2023, you're in for a treat. This guide will take you on a journey through Iceland's most breathtaking destinations, from the rugged highlands to the charming coastal towns. Whether you're looking to hike through the country's stunning national parks, take a dip in a geothermal pool, or discover the vibrant arts and music scene, this guide has got you covered.

We'll show you the best time to visit Iceland in 2023, along with tips and tricks to help you plan your itinerary, book your accommodations, and navigate the country's unique culture and customs. You'll learn about the best transportation options, the most popular tourist attractions, and the hidden gems that only the locals know about.

Our Iceland vacation guide for 2023 is designed to help you make the most of your trip, whether you're traveling solo, with a partner, or with the whole family. We'll give you practical advice on everything from packing and budgeting to safety and etiquette. You'll also get insider recommendations on the best restaurants, bars, and cafes to visit, as well as the top tours and activities to add to your itinerary.

So, what are you waiting for? Get ready to embark on the adventure of a lifetime and discover all that Iceland has to offer in 2023. With our comprehensive guide by your side, you'll be well-equipped to create memories that will last a lifetime.

Iceland is a breathtakingly beautiful country located in the North Atlantic Ocean, known for its stunning landscapes, geothermal activity, and unique culture. It is an ideal destination for first-time travelers for a multitude of reasons.

Firstly, Iceland is a safe and welcoming country with a low crime rate and a friendly, English-speaking population. This makes it an ideal destination for those who are new to traveling, as it offers a sense of security and comfort.

Secondly, Iceland's natural beauty is unparalleled. The country is home to some of the most stunning landscapes in the world, including glaciers, volcanoes, hot springs, and waterfalls. The rugged beauty of Iceland's landscape is truly awe-inspiring, and visitors can easily explore it on foot, by car, or on a guided tour.

Thirdly, Iceland is an excellent destination for outdoor enthusiasts. With a wide range of activities such as hiking, skiing, snowmobiling, whale watching, and horseback riding, there's something for everyone. For those who enjoy extreme sports, Iceland offers the opportunity to go ice climbing, glacier trekking, and even scuba diving in some of the world's clearest waters.

Fourthly, Iceland has a unique culture that is worth exploring. The country has a rich history and traditions that are reflected in its language, literature, and music. Visitors can experience Icelandic culture by attending festivals, trying local cuisine, or exploring the country's many museums and galleries.

Finally, Iceland is a convenient destination for first-time travelers. It is located relatively close to Europe and North America and has a well-developed tourism industry. The country's airports and ports are well-connected to major cities around the world, making it easy to get there and back.

In conclusion, Iceland is a perfect destination for first-time travelers. Its natural beauty, outdoor activities, unique culture, safety, and convenience make it an ideal place to visit. Whether you're looking for adventure or relaxation, Iceland has something for everyone.

WELCOME TO ICELAND: AN OVERVIEW OF YOUR ADVENTURE

Iceland, a Nordic island nation located in the North Atlantic, is an adventurer's paradise. Known for its stunning natural beauty, Iceland boasts a wide range of outdoor activities and unique experiences that are sure to captivate even the most seasoned traveler. Whether you are seeking the thrill of a lifetime or a more leisurely escape from the hustle and bustle of everyday life, Iceland has something to offer for everyone.

To start your adventure, you can explore Iceland's capital city of Reykjavik. This charming city is home to colorful houses, quaint cafes, and a vibrant arts and music scene. Take a stroll along the streets of the city center and admire the unique architecture, visit the famous Hallgrimskirkja church, or soak in one of the city's many geothermal hot springs.

But the true beauty of Iceland lies beyond the city limits. The island's natural wonders are nothing short of spectacular. From the towering glaciers to the powerful waterfalls, there are plenty of awe-inspiring sights to behold. One of the most popular destinations in Iceland is the Golden Circle, a 300-kilometer route that includes stops at the famous Geysir geothermal area, the Gullfoss waterfall, and the Thingvellir National Park.

For those looking for a bit more adventure, Iceland offers plenty of opportunities to explore its rugged terrain. Take a hike along the Laugavegur Trail, a 55-kilometer trek that passes through some of Iceland's most stunning landscapes, including glaciers, geothermal areas, and colorful mountains. Or, for a truly unique experience, try ice climbing on one of Iceland's glaciers.

If you prefer to take things at a slower pace, Iceland's geothermal hot springs are the perfect place to relax and unwind. The Blue Lagoon is one of the most popular hot springs in Iceland, offering warm, mineral-rich waters that are said to have healing properties. Other popular hot springs include the Secret Lagoon and the Myvatn Nature Baths.

And no trip to Iceland would be complete without a chance to see the Northern Lights. This spectacular natural phenomenon, also known as the Aurora Borealis, is visible from Iceland's dark skies from September to April. Join a guided tour to witness this stunning display of light and color firsthand.

In summary, Iceland is an adventurer's paradise, offering a wide range of outdoor activities and unique experiences. From exploring the city of Reykjavik to hiking through rugged terrain and soaking in geothermal hot springs, there is something for everyone in this beautiful Nordic island nation. So pack your bags and get ready for an unforgettable adventure in Iceland.

WHY ICELAND IS THE PERFECT DESTINATION FOR FIRST-TIMERS

Iceland is a Nordic island nation located in the North Atlantic Ocean, known for its stunning natural beauty, rugged landscapes, and unique culture. It is a perfect destination for first-time travelers who want to experience adventure, scenic beauty, and unique cultural experiences.

Here are some reasons why Iceland is the perfect destination for first-timers.

1. Safe Destination

Iceland is known to be one of the safest countries in the world, with a very low crime rate. This makes it a perfect destination for first-time travelers who are concerned about safety. Icelandic people are friendly and welcoming to visitors, making it an ideal place to explore without any worries.

2. Natural Beauty

Iceland is a land of spectacular natural beauty with its dramatic landscapes, glaciers, hot springs, waterfalls, and northern lights. It offers a unique opportunity to experience the raw and untouched nature. There are numerous outdoor activities to explore such as hiking, glacier walks, snowmobiling, and horse riding.

3. Easy to Navigate

Iceland is a small country, and its road network is easy to navigate, making it an ideal destination for first-time travelers. The roads are well-maintained and well-signed, and the public transport system is reliable, making it easy to get around. There are also guided tours available that take visitors to the most popular tourist destinations.

4. Unique Culture

Iceland has a unique culture that is influenced by its Viking heritage and isolation from mainland Europe. Icelandic people are proud of their cultural heritage, and visitors can experience it in many ways. For example, visitors can taste traditional Icelandic food, learn about Viking history, and visit museums that showcase Icelandic art and culture.

5. English-Speaking Nation

Icelanders speak English fluently, making it easy for first-time travelers to communicate with locals. This eliminates the language barrier and makes it easier to get around and explore the country. Additionally, many tourist destinations have English language signs and guides.

6. Affordable Destination

Iceland can be an affordable destination, depending on the time of year and the activities visitors choose to do. There are many budget-friendly options for accommodation and food, and many of the natural attractions are free to visit. Additionally, Iceland's currency, the Icelandic krona, has been historically weaker than major currencies, which can make it more affordable for tourists.

In conclusion, Iceland is the perfect destination for first-time travelers who want to experience adventure, natural beauty, and unique cultural experiences. It is a safe, easy-to-navigate, and English-speaking nation, with a unique culture and affordable options. Whether visitors want to explore the great outdoors or experience Icelandic culture, Iceland has something for everyone.

CHAPTER 1

PREPARING FOR YOUR TRIP

Preparing for a trip can be a daunting task, especially if it's your first time traveling or visiting a new destination. Proper preparation is key to ensuring a smooth and stress-free trip. Here are some tips to help you prepare for your trip.

1. Research Your Destination

Before you embark on your trip, research your destination thoroughly. Read up on the local culture, customs, traditions, and etiquette. This will help you understand and respect the local culture, which can make your trip more enjoyable.

Additionally, research the weather, currency exchange rates, and local transportation options.

2. Plan Your Itinerary

Planning your itinerary can help you make the most of your trip. Decide which attractions and activities you want to see and do, and allocate sufficient time for each. Make sure to include some downtime in your itinerary to avoid feeling overwhelmed or rushed.

3. Book Your Accommodation and Transportation

Book your accommodation and transportation in advance to avoid last-minute stress and higher prices. Use reputable websites and booking platforms, and read reviews to ensure that you're making a good choice. If you're traveling during peak season, book as early as possible to avoid disappointment.

4. Get Your Documents in Order

Make sure to have all your travel documents in order, including your passport, visas, and travel insurance. Check the expiry date of your passport and ensure that it's valid for at least six months beyond your planned travel dates. Additionally, check if you need a visa for your destination and obtain one if necessary. Finally, purchase travel insurance to protect yourself in case of unforeseen circumstances.

5. Pack Smartly

Packing smartly can help you avoid overpacking and reduce stress during your trip. Make a packing list and stick to it, packing only what you need. Consider the weather and activities you'll be doing, and pack accordingly. Additionally, pack a small carry-on bag with essentials such as medication, a change of clothes, and important documents in case your luggage is lost or delayed.

6. Notify Your Bank and Credit Card Company

Notify your bank and credit card company that you'll be traveling to avoid having your cards blocked due to suspicious activity. Inform them of your travel dates and destination, and ask about any fees or charges that may apply to international transactions.

7. Learn Some Basic Phrases

Learning some basic phrases in the local language can go a long way in making a good impression and improving your experience. Learn how to say hello, thank you, excuse me, and other common phrases. Additionally, carry a pocket dictionary or translation app to help you communicate in case of language barriers.

In conclusion, preparing for your trip is essential to ensure a smooth and stress-free experience. Research your destination, plan your itinerary, book your accommodation and transportation in advance, get your documents in order, pack smartly, notify your bank and credit card company, and learn some basic phrases. With proper preparation, you'll be able to enjoy your trip to the fullest.

PLANNING YOUR ICELAND VACATION: A STEP-BY-STEP GUIDE

Planning a vacation to Iceland can be an exciting and memorable experience. With its stunning natural beauty, unique culture, and friendly locals, Iceland is an ideal destination for travelers seeking adventure and exploration. Here's a step-by-step guide on how to plan your Iceland vacation:

1. Determine the best time to visit: Iceland's climate varies greatly depending on the time of year. Summer is the most popular time to visit, with mild temperatures and long daylight hours. However, winter can be just as magical, with the chance to see the Northern Lights and enjoy winter

activities such as ice caving and snowmobiling.

2. Decide on your itinerary: Iceland has so much to offer, from the famous Golden Circle to the remote Westfjords. Decide what sights and activities are a priority for you and plan your itinerary accordingly. Keep in mind that some attractions are only accessible during certain times of the year.

3. Book your flights and accommodations: Once you have determined the best time to visit and your itinerary, it's time to book your flights and accommodations. There are many options for accommodations in Iceland, from budget-friendly hostels to luxury hotels. Keep in mind that accommodations in popular areas can

book up quickly, especially during peak season.

4. Rent a car: Renting a car in Iceland is highly recommended, as it allows you the flexibility to explore at your own pace. Many of Iceland's most beautiful sights are off the beaten path and can only be reached by car. Be sure to book in advance and make sure you are familiar with Icelandic driving laws.

5. Plan for the weather: Iceland's weather can be unpredictable, even in the summer months. Be sure to pack clothing for a variety of conditions, including warm layers, rain gear, and sturdy shoes for hiking.

6. Research tours and activities: There are many guided tours and activities available in Iceland, from whale watching

to glacier hiking. Research and book in advance to ensure availability.

7. Learn about Icelandic culture: Iceland has a unique and fascinating culture, from its Viking heritage to its literary traditions. Take some time to learn about the culture and customs of Iceland before your trip to fully appreciate all that this amazing country has to offer.

ESSENTIAL ITEMS TO PACK FOR YOUR ICELAND ADVENTURE

Packing for a trip to Iceland requires careful consideration, as the weather and activities can be unpredictable. Here are some essential items to pack for your Iceland adventure:

1. Warm layers: Iceland's weather can be unpredictable, and temperatures can drop quickly. Be sure to pack warm layers, including a waterproof jacket, thermal underwear, and warm socks.

2. Sturdy shoes: Iceland's terrain can be rugged and rocky, so it's important to pack sturdy shoes with good grip for hiking and exploring.

3. Swimsuit: Iceland is known for its natural hot springs and geothermal pools, so be sure to pack a swimsuit for a relaxing soak.

4. Camera: Iceland's natural beauty is truly breathtaking, so be sure to bring a camera to capture all the amazing sights and memories.

5. Travel adapter: Iceland uses the European two-pronged plug, so be sure to bring a travel adapter if your electronics require a different plug type.

6. Portable charger: With all the sightseeing and activities you'll be doing, your phone battery is likely to drain quickly. Bring a portable charger to ensure you can stay connected and capture all the amazing moments.

7. Sunscreen and sunglasses: Even in the winter months, Iceland can experience bright sunlight, especially during the long summer days. Be sure to pack sunscreen and sunglasses to protect your skin and eyes.

8. Cash and credit card: Iceland is a cashless society, and credit cards are widely accepted. However, it's a good

idea to have some cash on hand for small purchases or in case of emergencies. It's also important to note that some remote areas may not accept credit cards, so having some cash can be helpful in these situations. Additionally, if you plan on using your credit card, be sure to let your bank know in advance to avoid any issues with fraud alerts.

CHAPTER 2

EXPLORING REYKJAVIK

Reykjavik is the capital and largest city of Iceland, a Nordic island country in the North Atlantic. The city is located on the southwestern coast of Iceland, and is known for its vibrant culture, colorful architecture, and natural beauty. It is the most populous city in Iceland, with a population of approximately 130,000 people.

In this article, we will explore the many attractions and activities that Reykjavik has to offer, from its museums and galleries, to its outdoor adventures and nightlife.

Museums and Galleries: Reykjavik is home to a number of world-class museums and galleries, which provide visitors with a glimpse into Iceland's rich cultural history and contemporary art scene. Here are some of the top museums and galleries in Reykjavik:

The National Museum of Iceland: The National Museum of Iceland is the country's largest museum, and houses a collection of artifacts and exhibits that chronicle Iceland's history from the settlement period to modern times. The museum's exhibits include Viking-era artifacts, religious objects, and displays on Icelandic folklore and culture.

The Reykjavik Art Museum: The Reykjavik Art Museum is the city's premier art museum, and features a collection of contemporary art from

Iceland and around the world. The museum has three locations in Reykjavik, each with its own distinct focus and collection.

The Icelandic Phallological Museum: The Icelandic Phallological Museum is a unique and somewhat controversial museum that houses a collection of over 280 penises and penile parts from mammals found in Iceland, including humans. The museum has become a popular attraction for tourists, and is known for its humorous and irreverent approach to the subject of human anatomy.

Outdoor Adventures: Reykjavik is also a great destination for outdoor enthusiasts, with plenty of opportunities for hiking, biking, and exploring Iceland's stunning natural landscapes. Here are some of the top outdoor adventures to experience in Reykjavik:

The Golden Circle: The Golden Circle is a popular tourist route that takes visitors on a tour of some of Iceland's most iconic natural landmarks, including the Geysir geothermal area, the Gullfoss waterfall, and Thingvellir National Park.

The Reykjanes Peninsula: The Reykjanes Peninsula is a rugged and otherworldly landscape that is home to Iceland's famous Blue Lagoon geothermal spa, as well as a number of hiking trails, volcanic craters, and lava fields.

Whale Watching: Reykjavik is one of the best places in the world for whale watching, with a number of tour operators offering boat tours to see humpback, minke, and killer whales in their natural habitat.

Nightlife: Reykjavik is also known for its vibrant and lively nightlife scene, with a wide range of bars, clubs, and music venues to suit every taste. Here are some of the top spots to check out:

Kaffibarinn: Kaffibarinn is a popular bar located in downtown Reykjavik, known for its cozy atmosphere and eclectic mix of music. The bar has become a popular spot for both locals and tourists, and is a great place to start a night out in Reykjavik.

Harpa Concert Hall: The Harpa Concert Hall is a stunning modern building that is home to the Iceland Symphony Orchestra and a range of other musical performances and events. The building's striking glass facade and stunning interior make it a must-visit attraction for music lovers.

Húrra: Húrra is a popular music venue and bar that hosts a range of live music performances, from indie rock to electronic and hip-hop. The venue has a lively and energetic atmosphere, and is a great place to experience Reykjavik's thriving music scene.

In conclusion, Reykjavik is a unique and fascinating city that offers a wide range of attractions and activities for visitors to enjoy. From its world-class museums and galleries, to its stunning natural landscapes and lively nightlife scene, there is something for everyone in this vibrant Nordic capital. Whether you're interested in exploring Iceland's rich cultural history, or immersing yourself in its breathtaking natural beauty, Reykjavik is a destination that is sure to leave a lasting impression.

REYKJAVIK: A CITY OF CONTRASTS AND CULTURE

Reykjavik, the capital of Iceland, is a city of contrasts and culture. It is a small, yet vibrant city with a population of around 130,000 people. The city is surrounded by mountains and sea, making it a unique location that offers natural beauty as well as urban attractions. Reykjavik is a city that prides itself on its cultural heritage, and it is reflected in the city's architecture, art, music, and literature.

Reykjavik is a city that is constantly evolving. It is a city that has seen significant growth in recent years, and as a result, it has become a hub for innovation and creativity. The city is home to a thriving startup scene, and it has a growing reputation as a hub for technology and innovation. The city's cultural scene is also flourishing, with a range of museums, galleries, and cultural events taking place throughout the year.

Despite its modern and cosmopolitan feel, Reykjavik remains deeply connected to its roots. Icelandic traditions and culture are still very much alive in the city, and they are celebrated in various forms throughout the year. From the annual Reykjavik Arts Festival to the Reykjavik Food and Fun Festival, there is always something going on in the city that celebrates Icelandic culture and heritage.

THE TOP THINGS TO SEE AND DO IN REYKJAVIK

Reykjavik is a city that is full of interesting things to see and do. From museums and galleries to natural wonders and outdoor activities, there is something for everyone in Reykjavik. Here are some of the top things to see and do in the city:

1. The National Museum of Iceland

The National Museum of Iceland is a must-visit destination for anyone interested in Icelandic history and culture. The museum's exhibits cover everything from the country's Viking past to its more recent history and culture. The museum also has a number of temporary exhibits that showcase the country's contemporary culture and art scene.

2. Hallgrimskirkja

Hallgrimskirkja is Reykjavik's iconic church, and it is one of the city's most recognizable landmarks. The church's impressive architecture and unique design make it a popular destination for tourists and locals alike. Visitors can climb to the top of the church tower for stunning views of the city.

3. The Blue Lagoon

The Blue Lagoon is one of Iceland's most famous attractions, and it is located just outside of Reykjavik. The lagoon is a natural geothermal spa that is known for its warm, milky blue waters. Visitors can relax in the warm waters, and take in the stunning surrounding scenery.

4. The Harpa Concert Hall

The Harpa Concert Hall is Reykjavik's premier music venue, and it is home to the Iceland Symphony Orchestra and the Icelandic Opera. The building's striking design and impressive acoustics make it a popular destination for music lovers.

5. The Reykjavik Art Museum

The Reykjavik Art Museum is home to a range of contemporary art exhibitions, as well as a collection of works by Icelandic artists. The museum's three locations offer a range of exhibits that showcase the country's vibrant art scene.

6. Whale Watching

Whale watching is a popular activity in Reykjavik, and there are a number of tour operators that offer whale watching trips. Visitors can see a variety of whale species, as well as other marine life, such as dolphins and seals.

7. The Golden Circle

The Golden Circle is a popular day trip from Reykjavik that takes visitors to some of Iceland's most famous natural attractions. The tour includes stops at the Geysir geothermal area, where visitors can see the famous Strokkur geyser erupting, as well as the stunning Gullfoss waterfall and the Þingvellir National Park, which is home to the site of Iceland's first parliament.

8. Reykjavik City Walk

A walking tour of Reykjavik is a great way to see the city's landmarks and learn about its history and culture. There are a number of tour operators that offer guided walking tours, or visitors can explore the city on their own using a map or guidebook.

9. The Aurora Borealis

The Aurora Borealis, also known as the Northern Lights, is a natural phenomenon that can be seen in Iceland during the winter months. Visitors can take a tour to see the lights, or venture out on their own to find a spot to view the spectacular light show.

10. The Perlan Museum

The Perlan Museum is a unique destination in Reykjavik that offers visitors a chance to learn about Iceland's natural wonders and unique environment. The museum's exhibits include a planetarium, an interactive glacier exhibit, and a viewing platform that offers stunning views of the city.

Overall, Reykjavik is a city that offers a wealth of attractions and activities for visitors to enjoy. Whether you're interested in history and culture, outdoor adventure, or just soaking in the stunning natural beauty of Iceland, there is something for everyone in this vibrant Nordic capital.

CHAPTER 3

NATURAL WONDERS OF ICELAND

Iceland, a Nordic island country located in the North Atlantic Ocean, is famous for its stunning landscapes, including glaciers, geysers, hot springs, waterfalls, and volcanoes. Iceland is known for its unique geological features, which are a result of its position on the Mid-Atlantic Ridge, a divergent tectonic boundary that separates the North American and Eurasian Plates. The country's natural wonders are a result of the interplay of volcanic activity, geothermal energy, glaciers, and the Atlantic Ocean. In this article, we will explore some of the most impressive natural wonders of Iceland.

1. The Northern Lights

One of the most spectacular natural wonders of Iceland is the Northern Lights, also known as the Aurora Borealis. This stunning display of light is caused by charged particles from the sun colliding with particles in the Earth's atmosphere. Iceland is an excellent location to view the Northern Lights due to its location near the Arctic Circle, where the lights are most visible. The best time to see the Northern Lights in Iceland is from September to April, although they can be seen as early as August and as late as May.

2. Geysers

Geysers are hot springs that periodically erupt with hot water and steam. Iceland is home to some of the world's most famous geysers, including the Great Geysir, which gives its name to all geysers worldwide. The Great Geysir is located in the Haukadalur Valley in southwest Iceland and has been erupting for thousands of years. Another famous geyser in Iceland is Strokkur, which erupts every 5-10 minutes, sending water up to 30 meters in the air.

3. Waterfalls
Iceland is home to many stunning waterfalls, including Gullfoss, Seljalandsfoss, and Skógafoss. Gullfoss, which translates to "Golden Falls," is one of Iceland's most famous waterfalls, and is located in the canyon of the Hvítá river in southwest Iceland. The waterfall drops 32 meters into a narrow canyon, creating a spectacular sight. Seljalandsfoss is a 60-meter high waterfall that drops over a rocky cliff. Visitors can walk behind the waterfall for a unique view. Skógafoss is another popular waterfall, located on the

Skógá River in southern Iceland. The waterfall drops 60 meters into a deep pool, and visitors can climb up to the top for a stunning view of the surrounding landscape.

4. Glacier Lagoons
Iceland is home to many stunning glacier lagoons, which are formed when glaciers melt and create pools of water. The most famous glacier lagoon in Iceland is Jökulsárlón, located in southeast Iceland. Jökulsárlón is a large lake filled with icebergs that have calved off from the Breiðamerkurjökull glacier. Visitors can take a boat tour to explore the lagoon and get up close to the icebergs. Another glacier lagoon in Iceland is Fjallsárlón, which is located nearby and is a smaller and quieter alternative to Jökulsárlón.

5. Hot Springs

Iceland is known for its many hot springs, which are a result of the country's geothermal activity. The most famous hot spring in Iceland is the Blue Lagoon, located in a lava field on the Reykjanes Peninsula. The Blue Lagoon is a geothermal spa that is heated by the nearby Svartsengi power plant. The water in the Blue Lagoon is rich in minerals, and many visitors come to bathe in the warm waters and enjoy the spa's many amenities. Other popular hot springs in Iceland include the Secret Lagoon, which is Iceland's oldest swimming pool, located in the town of Flúðir. The Secret Lagoon is a natural hot spring that has been modified for visitors, with a pool and changing facilities. Another popular hot spring in Iceland is Reykjadalur, which is located in a valley near the town of Hveragerði. Reykjadalur is a

3-kilometer hike from the town, and visitors can bathe in the warm waters of the river while enjoying the stunning surroundings.

6. Volcanoes
Iceland is home to over 30 active volcanic systems, making it a paradise for geologists and volcano enthusiasts. One of the most famous volcanoes in Iceland is Eyjafjallajökull, which erupted in 2010, causing widespread disruption to air travel in Europe. Another famous volcano is Hekla, which has erupted over 20 times since the year 874. Visitors can hike to the top of Hekla for a stunning view of the surrounding landscape.

7. Black Sand Beaches
Iceland's black sand beaches are a result of the country's volcanic activity, which creates a unique type of sand. The most

famous black sand beach in Iceland is Reynisfjara, located in southern Iceland. Reynisfjara is known for its dramatic basalt columns and towering sea stacks, which are a result of volcanic activity. Another popular black sand beach in Iceland is Diamond Beach, located near Jökulsárlón glacier lagoon. Diamond Beach is named for the many icebergs that wash up on its shore, creating a stunning contrast with the black sand.

8. Fjords
Iceland's fjords are a result of the country's unique geography, with its rugged coastline and numerous bays and inlets. One of the most famous fjords in Iceland is Eyjafjörður, located in northern Iceland. Eyjafjörður is Iceland's longest fjord and is known for its stunning scenery and abundant wildlife. Another popular fjord in Iceland is

Ísafjörður, located in the Westfjords region. Ísafjörður is a small town surrounded by towering mountains and offers visitors a chance to explore Iceland's remote and wild landscape.

In conclusion, Iceland is a country that offers visitors a unique and stunning array of natural wonders, from the Northern Lights to its glaciers, volcanoes, hot springs, waterfalls, black sand beaches, and fjords. The country's unique geology, which is a result of its location on the Mid-Atlantic Ridge, has created a landscape that is unlike any other in the world. Whether you are interested in hiking, photography, or simply soaking in a hot spring, Iceland has something to offer everyone.

THE GOLDEN CIRCLE: A ROAD TRIP THROUGH ICELAND'S NATURAL BEAUTY

The Golden Circle is a popular road trip route in Iceland that takes visitors to some of the country's most stunning natural wonders. The route starts and ends in Reykjavik and covers approximately 300 kilometers. The three main stops on the Golden Circle are Þingvellir National Park, the Geysir Geothermal Area, and the Gullfoss waterfall.

Þingvellir National Park is a UNESCO World Heritage Site and is located in a rift valley where the North American and Eurasian tectonic plates meet. Visitors can walk along the Mid-Atlantic Ridge, where the plates are pulling apart, and see the site where Iceland's parliament was founded in the year 930. The park is also home to the crystal-clear Þingvallavatn Lake, which is a popular spot for fishing and snorkeling.

The Geysir Geothermal Area is located in the Haukadalur valley and is home to the Strokkur geyser, which erupts every 5-10 minutes, shooting water up to 30 meters in the air. Visitors can walk around the geothermal area and see the various hot springs and bubbling mud pots.

Gullfoss waterfall, also known as the "Golden Falls," is one of Iceland's most iconic waterfalls. The waterfall is located on the Hvítá river and drops 32 meters into a narrow canyon. Visitors can walk along a path that takes them right up to the edge of the waterfall, where they can feel the mist on their face and see the rainbows that form in the mist.

In addition to the three main stops, there are several other attractions along the Golden Circle route, including the Kerið volcanic crater lake and the Friðheimar greenhouse, where visitors can see how tomatoes are grown using geothermal energy.

EXPLORING ICELAND'S GLACIERS: AN ADVENTURE OF A LIFETIME

Iceland is home to several glaciers, including the Vatnajökull glacier, which is the largest glacier in Europe. Exploring Iceland's glaciers is an unforgettable experience, and there are several ways to do it.

One of the most popular ways to explore Iceland's glaciers is by taking a guided glacier hike. Visitors can hike on the glacier with a guide, who will provide the necessary equipment, such as crampons and ice axes, and teach them about the glacier's formation and history. Visitors can also take a snowmobile tour on the glacier, which is an exhilarating way to see the vast expanse of ice.

Another popular activity on Iceland's glaciers is ice caving. During the winter months, ice caves form in the glacier, and visitors can explore these stunning natural formations. Visitors can take a guided ice cave tour, where they will be led into the caves and provided with the necessary equipment.

For those looking for a truly unique experience, there are also helicopter tours of Iceland's glaciers. Visitors can take a helicopter ride over the glaciers and see the stunning landscape from above.

THE NORTHERN LIGHTS: CHASING AURORA BOREALIS IN ICELAND

The Northern Lights, also known as Aurora Borealis, are a natural phenomenon that occurs when charged particles from the sun collide with the Earth's atmosphere. Iceland is one of the best places in the world to see the Northern Lights, and there are several ways to experience this incredible natural wonder.

One of the most popular ways to see the Northern Lights in Iceland is by taking a guided tour. Visitors can book a tour with a local guide, who will take them to the best spots for viewing the Northern Lights and provide them with information about the science behind the phenomenon.

For those who want a more immersive experience, there are also few options available. Visitors can stay in a remote cabin or hotel in the countryside, where they will have a better chance of seeing the Northern Lights away from the light pollution of the city. Some hotels even offer wake-up calls if the Northern Lights appear during the night.

Another unique way to experience the Northern Lights is by taking a boat tour. Visitors can take a boat out into the ocean, away from the city lights, and see the Northern Lights dancing above them. The reflections of the lights on the water create a truly magical experience.

For those who want to capture the Northern Lights on camera, there are also photography tours available. Visitors can take a tour with a professional photographer, who will teach them how to capture the Northern Lights in the best possible way.

It's important to note that the Northern Lights are a natural phenomenon, and there is no guarantee that they will appear on any given night. However, with the right conditions and a bit of luck, visitors to Iceland have a good chance of seeing this incredible display of nature.

RELAXING IN ICELAND'S HOT SPRINGS AND SPAS

Iceland is known for its many hot springs, which are a result of the country's geothermal activity. The most famous hot spring in Iceland is the Blue Lagoon, located in a lava field on the Reykjanes Peninsula. The Blue Lagoon is a geothermal spa that is heated by the nearby Svartsengi power plant. The water in the Blue Lagoon is rich in minerals, and many visitors come to bathe in the warm waters and enjoy the spa's many amenities.

Other popular hot springs in Iceland include the Secret Lagoon, located in

Flúðir, which is Iceland's oldest swimming pool and a great place to relax after a long day of exploring. The Mývatn Nature Baths, located in the north of Iceland, are another popular geothermal spa and offer stunning views of the surrounding landscape.

In addition to hot springs, Iceland is also home to several world-class spas. The most famous of these is the Blue Lagoon Spa, which offers a range of treatments and therapies, including massages, facials, and body scrubs. Other popular spas in Iceland include the Laugar Spa in Reykjavik and the Geo Spa at the Deildartunguhver hot spring.

In addition to their relaxing qualities, Iceland's hot springs and spas are also known for their therapeutic benefits. The warm water and minerals are said to help alleviate stress, ease muscle pain, and improve skin conditions.

Overall, Iceland offers a unique and unforgettable experience for those looking to connect with nature and relax in stunning surroundings. From the natural wonders of the Golden Circle to the thrilling adventures of exploring glaciers, to the magical experience of chasing the Northern Lights, to the soothing qualities of the country's hot springs and spas, Iceland has something for everyone.

CHAPTER 4

BEYOND REYKJAVIK: EXPLORING ICELAND'S REGIONS

Iceland is a country of natural beauty, with unique landscapes and geological features that can be found throughout its various regions. While the capital city of Reykjavik is a popular starting point for many visitors, there is so much more to explore beyond the city limits. In this article, we will take a closer look at some of Iceland's regions and the attractions that can be found within them.

1. West Iceland

West Iceland is a region that is characterized by its rugged coastline, volcanic craters, and picturesque fjords. One of the main attractions in this area is the Snaefellsnes Peninsula, which is often referred to as "Iceland in Miniature" because of its diverse range of landscapes. Visitors to the peninsula can explore black sand beaches, fishing villages, and the iconic Snaefellsjokull glacier.

Another popular attraction in West Iceland is the Hraunfossar waterfalls, which are a series of cascading waterfalls that flow from beneath a lava field. Nearby, visitors can also explore the historical site of Reykholt, which was the home of Iceland's most famous medieval writer, Snorri Sturluson.

2. North Iceland

North Iceland is a region that is known for its dramatic landscapes and geothermal activity. One of the main attractions in this area is the Lake Myvatn region, which is home to a diverse range of geological features, including bubbling mud pools, steaming fumaroles, and the dramatic Hverfjall crater.

Another popular attraction in North Iceland is the Godafoss waterfall, which is one of the country's most impressive waterfalls. The waterfall is named after the pagan gods that were worshipped in Iceland before Christianity, and it is said that the lawspeaker of the Icelandic parliament threw his pagan idols into the waterfall when he converted to Christianity in the year 1000.

3. East Iceland

East Iceland is a region that is characterized by its rugged mountains, glaciers, and remote fishing villages. One of the main attractions in this area is the Vatnajokull glacier, which is the largest glacier in Europe. Visitors to the area can explore the glacier on foot, take a snowmobile tour, or even go ice climbing.

Another popular attraction in East Iceland is the town of Seydisfjordur, which is known for its picturesque harbor, colorful houses, and vibrant arts scene. The town is home to several art galleries, music venues, and craft shops, and it is also the starting point for several hiking trails in the surrounding mountains.

4. South Iceland

South Iceland is a region that is known for its glaciers, waterfalls, and black sand beaches. One of the main attractions in this area is the Vatnajokull glacier, which is the largest glacier in Europe. Visitors to the area can explore the glacier on foot, take a snowmobile tour, or even go ice climbing.

Another popular attraction in South Iceland is the town of Vik, which is located on the southern coast of Iceland. The town is known for its black sand beaches, dramatic sea stacks, and towering cliffs. Visitors to Vik can explore the town's many hiking trails, take a boat tour to see the local puffin colonies, or simply relax and take in the stunning scenery.

5. Westfjords

The Westfjords region is a remote and sparsely populated area that is known for its rugged landscapes, deep fjords, and abundant wildlife. One of the main attractions in this area is the Hornstrandir Nature Reserve, which is a remote and uninhabited wilderness area that is only accessible by boat or on foot. Visitors to the reserve can explore the area's many hiking trails, spot local wildlife, and enjoy the stunning views of the surrounding mountains and coastline. The Westfjords are also home to several charming fishing villages, such as Isafjordur and Patreksfjordur, where visitors can learn about the area's rich maritime history and sample fresh seafood.

Another popular attraction in the Westfjords is the Dynjandi waterfall, which is one of the country's most impressive waterfalls. The waterfall is actually a series of cascading waterfalls, and visitors can hike to the top of the falls for stunning views of the surrounding landscape.

6. Reykjanes Peninsula

The Reykjanes Peninsula is a region that is located in the southwest corner of Iceland, near the capital city of Reykjavik. The area is known for its geothermal activity and unique landscapes, including the famous Blue Lagoon spa.

One of the main attractions in the Reykjanes Peninsula is the Gunnuhver hot spring, which is a powerful geothermal area that features boiling mud pots and steam vents. Visitors to the area can also explore the nearby Krýsuvík geothermal field, which features a colorful landscape of bubbling mud pools and steaming vents.

Another popular attraction in the Reykjanes Peninsula is the Bridge Between Continents, which is a small footbridge that spans a rift between the Eurasian and North American tectonic plates. Visitors can walk across the bridge and learn about the geological forces that have shaped Iceland's unique landscapes.

In conclusion, Iceland is a country that is full of natural wonders and unique landscapes. From the rugged coastline of West Iceland to the remote wilderness of the Westfjords, there is something for every type of traveler. Whether you prefer hiking, wildlife spotting, or relaxing in hot springs, Iceland has it all. So pack your bags and get ready to explore this fascinating country!

Iceland is a land of breathtaking landscapes, rugged terrain, and natural wonders. Each region of the country has its own unique charm and beauty, from the geysers and hot springs of the southwest to the glaciers and fjords of the north. In this article, we'll explore four of Iceland's most captivating regions: the Westfjords, the South Coast, the Eastfjords, and the North.

THE WESTFJORDS: ICELAND'S HIDDEN GEM

Located in the northwestern corner of Iceland, the Westfjords are one of the country's most remote and least-visited regions. This rugged peninsula is home to some of Iceland's most stunning natural wonders, including dramatic cliffs, deep fjords, and picturesque fishing villages.

One of the Westfjords' most iconic landmarks is the towering bird cliffs of Látrabjarg. This 14-kilometer-long cliff face is home to millions of seabirds, including puffins, guillemots, and razorbills. Visitors can hike along the cliff tops for a chance to see these amazing creatures up close.

Another must-see attraction in the Westfjords is the Dynjandi waterfall. This magnificent waterfall cascades down a series of rocky steps, creating a mesmerizing display of water and mist. Visitors can hike to the top of the falls for an even more spectacular view.

For those interested in Icelandic history and culture, the Westfjords are also home to several museums and cultural sites. The Ísafjörður Maritime Museum explores the region's rich seafaring history, while the Icelandic Sea Monster Museum offers a unique look at the folklore and legends of the area.

THE SOUTH COAST: WATERFALLS, BLACK SAND BEACHES, AND MORE

The South Coast of Iceland is one of the country's most popular tourist destinations, and it's easy to see why. This region is home to some of Iceland's most stunning natural wonders, including towering waterfalls, dramatic glaciers, and black sand beaches.

One of the most famous attractions in the South Coast is the Skógafoss waterfall. This 60-meter-tall waterfall is one of the largest in Iceland, and visitors can hike to the top of the falls for a spectacular view of the surrounding landscape.

Another must-see attraction in the South Coast is the Jökulsárlón glacier lagoon.

This stunning glacial lake is filled with icebergs, and visitors can take a boat tour to get up close and personal with these amazing natural sculptures.

For those interested in Icelandic history, the South Coast is also home to several museums and cultural sites. The Skógar Museum offers a fascinating look at Icelandic folklore and tradition, while the Vatnajökull Glacier Visitor Centre provides insight into the region's geology and natural history.

THE EASTFJORDS: REMOTE BEAUTY AND SERENITY

The Eastfjords of Iceland are some of the most remote and least-visited regions of the country. This rugged coastline is home to picturesque fishing villages, stunning mountain landscapes, and pristine fjords.

One of the most iconic landmarks in the Eastfjords is the towering mountain of Snæfell. This majestic peak is the highest mountain in the region, and visitors can hike to the top for an incredible view of the surrounding landscape.

Another must-see attraction in the Eastfjords is the town of Seyðisfjörður. This picturesque village is nestled in a narrow fjord and is home to several art galleries, museums, and cultural events throughout the year.

For those interested in Icelandic history and culture, the Eastfjords are also home to several museums and cultural sites. The East Iceland Heritage Museum provides a fascinating look at the region's history, from Viking settlements to modern times. The museum's collection includes artifacts and exhibits on topics such as fishing, farming, and local traditions. Another cultural site in the Eastfjords is the Petra Stone Collection in Stöðvarfjörður, which showcases a unique collection of rocks and minerals gathered by the late Petra Sveinsdóttir throughout her lifetime.

THE NORTH: A LAND OF CONTRASTS AND CULTURE

The North of Iceland is a region of contrasts, from the rolling hills and verdant valleys of the south to the stark volcanic landscapes of the north. This region is home to some of Iceland's most iconic natural wonders, including the

Mývatn geothermal area, the Goðafoss waterfall, and the Vatnajökull glacier.

One of the most unique attractions in the North is the Hverfjall crater. This massive volcanic crater is over a kilometer wide and provides visitors with an otherworldly experience as they hike to the top for an incredible view of the surrounding landscape.

Another must-see attraction in the North is the town of Akureyri. This vibrant city is known as the "capital of the North" and is home to several museums, art galleries, and cultural events throughout the year. Visitors can explore the Akureyri Botanical Garden, which features plants from all over the world, or take a stroll along the city's charming streets and colorful houses.

For those interested in Icelandic history and culture, the North is also home to several museums and cultural sites. The Laufás turf farm offers a glimpse into traditional Icelandic architecture and lifestyle, while the Húsavík Whale Museum explores the region's rich maritime history and the importance of whales to Icelandic culture.

In conclusion, Iceland is a land of stunning natural beauty, rich culture, and fascinating history. Each region of the country has its own unique charm and attractions, from the remote and rugged Westfjords to the vibrant and cultural North. Whether you're interested in hiking, history, or just taking in the incredible scenery, Iceland has something for everyone.

CHAPTER 5

PRACTICAL INFORMATION FOR YOUR ICELAND VACATION

If you're planning a trip to Iceland, there are several practical things you should keep in mind before your arrival. From transportation to accommodations, here's a guide to some of the most important things to know when planning your Iceland vacation.

Transportation:

One of the best ways to get around Iceland is by renting a car. This will allow you to explore the country at your own pace and stop wherever you want along the way. Many of the popular tourist destinations are located outside of the main cities, so having your own car is essential. There are several car rental companies to choose from in Iceland, and it's recommended to book in advance to ensure availability.

If you prefer not to drive, there are also several bus companies that operate throughout the country. The most popular bus company is Reykjavik Excursions, which offers several tours and routes to different parts of Iceland.

Accommodations:

There are several options for accommodations in Iceland, ranging from budget-friendly hostels to luxurious hotels. It's recommended to book accommodations in advance, especially during peak tourist season

(June-August). Some popular websites to search for accommodations in Iceland include Booking.com, Airbnb, and Hostelworld.

If you're looking for a unique experience, there are several options for staying in Iceland's countryside, such as staying in a traditional Icelandic farmhouse or a cozy cabin.

Food:

Icelandic cuisine is known for its fresh seafood, lamb, and unique delicacies such as fermented shark and sheep's head. If you're a foodie, there are several restaurants in Reykjavik and throughout the country that offer traditional Icelandic dishes. Keep in mind that eating out in Iceland can be expensive, so it's recommended to budget accordingly.

If you're on a budget or prefer to cook your own meals, there are several grocery stores throughout the country, such as Bónus and Krónan. It's also recommended to try some of Iceland's unique snacks, such as licorice-flavored chocolate and dried fish.

Weather:

Iceland's weather can be unpredictable, so it's recommended to pack accordingly. Even during the summer months, it can be chilly and rainy, so it's recommended to bring warm layers and waterproof clothing. If you're planning on hiking or spending time outdoors, it's important to have sturdy footwear.

During the winter months, Iceland experiences limited daylight hours and snowy conditions. If you're planning on visiting Iceland during the winter, it's recommended to bring warm clothing and consider taking a guided tour for safety.

Money:

Iceland's currency is the Icelandic króna (ISK). Credit cards are widely accepted throughout the country, but it's recommended to have some cash on hand for smaller purchases or if you're visiting more remote areas. It's also recommended to notify your bank before traveling to Iceland to avoid any issues with your credit card.

Language:

The official language of Iceland is Icelandic, but English is widely spoken throughout the country, especially in tourist areas. It's still recommended to learn some basic Icelandic phrases, such as "takk fyrir" (thank you) and "bless" (goodbye).

Safety:

Iceland is a safe country to travel in, but it's still important to take precautions while exploring. When hiking or spending time outdoors, it's recommended to stay on marked trails and be aware of weather conditions. If you're driving, it's important to be aware of road conditions and take caution on narrow, winding roads.

In case of emergency, the emergency number in Iceland is 112.

In conclusion, planning a trip to Iceland can be an exciting and memorable experience. By keeping these practical tips in mind, you can ensure a safe and enjoyable trip while exploring the stunning natural beauty and rich culture of Iceland.

GETTING AROUND ICELAND: TRANSPORTATION OPTIONS

Renting a Car:

One of the best ways to get around Iceland is by renting a car. This will allow you to explore the country at your own pace and stop wherever you want along the way. Many of the popular tourist destinations are located outside of the main cities, so having your own car is essential. There are several car rental companies to choose from in Iceland, and it's recommended to book in advance to ensure availability.

Keep in mind that Iceland's roads can be challenging, especially during the winter months. It's important to have experience driving in snowy and icy conditions and to choose a vehicle with four-wheel drive.

Taking the Bus:

If you prefer not to drive, there are also several bus companies that operate throughout the country. The most popular bus company is Reykjavik Excursions, which offers several tours and routes to different parts of Iceland.

The bus system in Iceland is reliable and efficient, with buses running on a regular schedule throughout the day. However, it's important to note that some destinations may not be accessible by bus, especially if you're looking to explore the country's more remote areas.

Flying:

Another transportation option in Iceland is flying. Iceland has several domestic airports that connect to different parts of the country, making it a convenient way to travel if you're short on time or looking to explore more remote areas.

The main domestic airline in Iceland is Air Iceland Connect, which offers several daily flights to different parts of the country. Keep in mind that flying can be more expensive than other transportation options and may not be practical if you're traveling on a budget.

WHERE TO STAY IN ICELAND: A GUIDE TO ACCOMMODATION

Hotels:

Iceland has several hotels to choose from, ranging from budget-friendly options to luxurious accommodations. If you're looking for a comfortable and convenient place to stay, hotels are a great option.

Some popular hotels in Iceland include the Fosshotel chain, which has several locations throughout the country, and the Icelandair Hotels chain, which is known for its comfortable accommodations and convenient locations.

Hostels:

If you're on a budget or looking for a more social atmosphere, hostels are a great option. Iceland has several hostels to choose from, ranging from basic accommodations to more upscale options.

Some popular hostels in Iceland include Kex Hostel in Reykjavik, which is known for its hip atmosphere and lively social scene, and Akureyri Backpackers in the north, which is a great base for exploring the region's natural beauty.

Camping:

If you're looking for a more rustic experience, camping is a great option in Iceland. The country has several campsites to choose from, ranging from basic facilities to more upscale options with hot tubs and other amenities.

Keep in mind that camping in Iceland can be challenging, especially during the winter months. It's important to have the right gear and to be prepared for the country's unpredictable weather conditions.

TIPS FOR SAFE AND RESPONSIBLE TRAVEL IN ICELAND

Respect the Environment:

Iceland's natural beauty is one of its biggest draws, but it's important to be responsible and respectful when exploring the country's wilderness areas. This means staying on marked trails, packing out your trash, and avoiding disturbing wildlife.

Be Prepared for the Weather:

Iceland's weather can be unpredictable, so it's important to be prepared for sudden changes in conditions. This means bringing warm layers, waterproof clothing, and sturdy shoes, even if you're visiting during the summer months.

It's also important to check the weather forecast regularly and to be prepared for road closures or other travel disruptions in the event of extreme weather.

Drive Safely:

If you're renting a car in Iceland, it's important to drive safely and responsibly. Iceland's roads can be challenging, especially during the winter months, so it's important to have experience driving in snowy and icy conditions.

Be sure to follow posted speed limits and to use caution when driving on gravel roads or near cliff edges. It's also important to stay alert for wildlife on the roads, especially in more remote areas.

Respect Local Customs and Traditions:

Iceland has a unique culture and set of traditions, and it's important to be respectful of these when visiting the country. This means dressing appropriately for cultural and religious sites, following local customs and etiquette, and being mindful of noise levels in residential areas.

It's also important to be respectful of the country's fragile ecosystems and to avoid damaging sensitive areas, such as moss-covered lava fields.

In conclusion, Iceland is a country with incredible natural beauty and a unique culture and history. Whether you're exploring the country's stunning landscapes, soaking in its hot springs, or immersing yourself in its vibrant art and music scene, there are several transportation and accommodation options to suit your needs. By following these tips for safe and responsible travel, you can enjoy all that Iceland has to offer while minimizing your impact on its delicate ecosystems and cultural heritage.

CONCLUSION

In conclusion, Iceland is a breathtaking country that offers some of the most unique and unforgettable travel experiences in the world. Whether you are a first-time visitor or a seasoned traveler, Iceland is a destination that should be on everyone's bucket list.

With its stunning natural landscapes, geothermal hot springs, waterfalls, glaciers, and wildlife, Iceland offers something for everyone. And with this comprehensive travel guide, you can rest assured that you will have all the information you need to plan an unforgettable vacation in Iceland in 2023.

From the best time to visit and the must-see attractions to the top accommodations and activities, this guide has everything you need to make the most of your Iceland vacation. Whether you want to relax in a natural hot spring, hike to a glacier, or watch the Northern Lights dance across the sky, Iceland has it all.

So if you're looking for an adventure of a lifetime, Iceland is the perfect destination. And with this travel guide, you'll have everything you need to discover the best of Iceland in 2023. So pack your bags, get ready to explore, and let Iceland amaze you with its natural wonders and incredible culture.

WRAPPING UP YOUR ICELAND VACATION: MEMORIES TO LAST A LIFETIME

As your Iceland vacation draws to a close, you'll likely find yourself reflecting on the incredible experiences and memories you've made during your time here. From the stunning natural beauty to the unique culture and friendly locals, Iceland is a destination that has something to offer everyone.

Whether you've spent your days exploring the rugged terrain of the Icelandic wilderness, soaking in a natural hot spring, or immersing yourself in the vibrant arts and culture scene, your time in Iceland is sure to be filled with unforgettable moments.

As you pack your bags and prepare to say goodbye to this magical country, take a moment to reflect on some of the highlights of your trip. Perhaps it was the breathtaking views of the Northern Lights dancing across the night sky, the exhilaration of hiking up to a glacier, or the peaceful relaxation of soaking in a hot spring under the stars.

Whatever your favorite memories may be, be sure to take some time to savor them and reflect on the unique experiences that you've had during your time in Iceland.

Before you depart, there are a few final things you may want to consider to make the most of your time in Iceland and ensure that your memories of this incredible country will last a lifetime.

First, be sure to take plenty of photographs and videos of your experiences. Whether you're snapping pictures of the stunning landscapes, capturing the essence of Icelandic culture, or simply taking selfies with your new friends, these photos will be invaluable in helping you relive your memories of Iceland long after you've returned home.

Second, consider picking up some souvenirs to remind you of your time in Iceland. Whether it's a traditional Icelandic sweater, a piece of unique jewelry crafted by a local artisan, or a bottle of delicious Icelandic schnapps, these souvenirs will serve as tangible reminders of the incredible experiences you had during your trip.

Finally, don't forget to take some time to say goodbye to Iceland and all that it has to offer. Whether it's taking a final hike, visiting a local museum, or simply spending some time wandering the streets of Reykjavik, take some time to soak in the sights, sounds, and sensations of this amazing country before you depart.

In the end, your Iceland vacation will undoubtedly be a once-in-a-lifetime experience that you will cherish for years to come. From the stunning natural beauty to the unique culture and friendly locals, Iceland has a way of capturing the hearts and imaginations of all who visit.

So as you wrap up your Iceland vacation, take some time to savor the memories and reflect on the incredible experiences you've had. And remember, no matter where your travels may take you in the future, Iceland will always hold a special place in your heart.

Printed in Great Britain
by Amazon